For a better life
Thought

A Book on Self-Empowerment

Compiled by
M. M. Walia

NEW DAWN PRESS, INC.
USA • UK • INDIA

NEW DAWN PRESS GROUP

Published by New Dawn Press Group
New Dawn Press, Inc., 244 South Randall Rd # 90, Elgin, IL 60123
e-mail: sales@newdawnpress.com

New Dawn Press, 2 Tintern Close, Slough, Berkshire, SL1-2TB, UK
e-mail: salesuk@newdawnpress.org

New Dawn Press (An Imprint of Sterling Publishers (P) Ltd)
A-59, Okhla Industrial Area, Phase-II, New Delhi-110020, India
e-mail: info@sterlingpublishers.com
www.sterlingpublishers.com

For a better life – Thought

© 2006, Sterling Publishers (P) Ltd
ISBN 1 84557 581 4

All rights are reserved. No part of this publication may be reproduced, stored in a retrieval system or transmitted, in any form or by any means, mechanical, photocopying, recording or otherwise, without prior written permission of the publisher.

PRINTED IN INDIA

Positive Thinking

"If you THINK you are beaten, you are.
If you THINK you dare not, you don't.
If you'd like to win
but THINK you can't,
It's almost certain you won't.
Life's winnings don't always go
   to the strongest and fastest man;
Sooner or later the man who wins
   is the man who THINKS he can."
       – Hugh R Wright

The powerful influence thoughts have on one's personality, as also their impact on the environment in general, is phenomenal. Thus, pure and positive thoughts generate calm and happiness all around.

*"Think positive...
the rest will follow"
– Guruvarya Param Pujya Saheb*

The faculty to think is perhaps the most powerful attribute of the mind. The ability to discriminate between the good and bad is the finest element of this unique human trait.

Thought Force – Its Physics and its Philosophy

- You can move the world through thought-force. Thought has great power. It can be transmitted from one man to another man.

- Thoughts can heal diseases. They can transform the mentality of persons. Thoughts can work wonders.

- He who has pure thoughts speaks very powerfully, and produces deep impressions on the minds of the listeners.

- A pure thought is sharper than the edge of a razor. Always entertain pure, sublime thoughts.
- One should be in tune with the mental vibrations or thought-vibrations of another. Only then can one easily understand another.
- Do not store in your brain useless information. Learn to unwind the mind. Unlearn whatever is of no use to you.
- Every impulse of the mind, every thought, is conveyed to the body cells. They are greatly influenced by

the varying conditions of the states of the mind. If there is confusion, depression and other negative emotions in the mind, they are telegraphically transmitted through the nerves to every cell in the body which then become inefficient.

Man often becomes what he believes himself to be. If I keep on saying to myself that I cannot do a certain thing, it is possible that I may end up by really becoming incapable of doing it. On the contrary, if I have the belief that I can do it, I shall surely acquire the capacity to do it, even if I may not have it at the beginning.

– Mahatma Gandhi

Thoughts Chisel Your Countenance

- ❖ Your face is like a gramophone record or plate. Whatever you think is at once written on your face.

- ❖ The face is the index of the mind. It is the mould of the mind. Every thought cuts a groove in the face. A divine thought brightens the face. An evil thought darkens the face. Continued evil thoughts increase the depth of dark impressions. Continued divine thoughts increase the aura on the face.

Thoughts – The Architect of Destiny

- If the mind dwells continually upon a train of thought, a groove is formed into which the thought-force runs automatically.

- Every action has a past which leads up to it; every action has a future which proceeds from it. An action implies a desire which prompted it and a thought which shaped it.

- Not easy is the act of explaining the detailed workings of thought and destiny. Every Karma produces a two-fold effect, one on the individual mind and the other on the world.

❖ Man is the master of his own destiny. By the power of your thought, you yourself make your destiny.

Your Eyes Betray Your Thoughts

- ❖ Your eyes represent the windows of your soul and bespeak the condition and state of your mind.

- ❖ If you have the faculty to read the eyes of others, you can read the mind at once. You can read the uppermost thought of a man if you are careful to mark the signs on his face, in his conversation and behaviour.

Negative Thoughts Poison Life

❖ Thoughts of worry and thoughts of fear are fearful forces within us. They poison the very sources of life and destroy the harmony, the running efficiency, the vitality and vigour. On the contrary, thoughts of cheerfulness, joy and courage, heal and soothe, and multiply mental powers. Be cheerful always.

Psycho-Physical Imbalances

❖ Thoughts exert influence over the body. Grief weakens the body. The body influences the mind too. A healthy body makes a healthy mind.

❖ Violent fits of hot temper do serious damage to the brain-cells, release poisonous chemical products into the blood, produce general shock and depression, drains away your energy and vitality, induces premature old age and shortens life.

- ❖ Thought creates the world. Thought brings things into existence.
- ❖ Think of a person as a good friend of yours and it becomes a reality. Think of him as your foe, and the mind perfects the thought into an actuality.

Similar Thoughts Attract Each Other

❖ In the thought-world also, the great law "Like attracts like" operates. People of similar thoughts are attracted towards each other. That is the reason why the maxims run as follows : "Birds of the same feather flock together"; "A man is known by the company he keeps".

Thoughts are Contagious

- ❖ It may be remembered that thought is very contagious.
- ❖ A cheerful thought in you produces cheerful thoughts in others.

The Application of the Psychological Law

- Keep the heart young. Do not think: "I have become old". To think so is a bad habit. As you think, so you become.

- "As a man thinketh so he becometh." This is a great truth or truism. Think, "I am strong", strong you become. Think, "I am a sage", sage you become.

- Thought has tremendous force. Your present is the result of your past thoughts, and your future will be according to your present thoughts. If you think rightly, you will speak rightly and act rightly. Speech and action simply follow the thoughts.

Higher Thoughts

- ❖ As are your thoughts, so must be your life. Improve your thinking. Better thoughts bring better actions.

- ❖ Food forms the mind very subtly. Food does not mean merely what we eat, but what we gather through all our senses.

- ❖ You can see better, hear better, taste better, think better when you entertain sublime, divine thoughts.

- ❖ Free yourself from the slavery of prejudice that blunts the intellect and dulls thought.

Thought – A Boomerang

- Be careful with your thoughts. Whatever you send out of your mind, comes back to you. Every thought you think, is a boomerang.
- If you hate another, hate will come back to you. If you love others, love will come back to you.
- An evil thought is thrice cursed. Firstly, it harms the thinker by doing injury to his mental body. Secondly, it harms the person who is its object. Lastly, it harms all mankind by vitiating the whole mental atmosphere.

Influence of Saintly Thoughts

- ❖ When we go and sit near a sage, we feel a unique calmness; but if we are in the company of a bad and selfish person, we feel uneasy. This is because the vibrations of peace and calmness emanate from the aura of the sage, whereas from the aura of the selfish person emanate vibrations of evil and selfish thoughts.

- ❖ We are always surrounded by these thought-forms and our minds are seriously affected by them. Not one-fourth of our thoughts are our own, but are simply picked up from the atmosphere. Mostly, they are of an evil nature. So we should always utter God's name mentally. It will always protect us from their evil influence.

- ❖ Whatever the Mind of man can conceive and believe, it can achieve it.

  – *Napolean Hill*

- ❖ Both poverty and riches are the offsprings of Thought.

  – *Napolean Hill*

- ❖ Confucius said, "If out of the three hundred songs I had to take one phrase to cover all my teachings, I would say, Let there be no evil in your thoughts."

  – *Analects*

Serve Others by Thought-Vibrations

Pure, strong thought-vibrations from saints travel a very long distance, purify the world and enter the minds of many thousands of persons.

Doctors Can Heal by Suggestions

Good and powerful suggestions can cure any disease. This healing by suggestion is a drugless treatment. It is suggestive therapeutics.

Yogins Preach by Thought-Transference

❖ Great souls transmit their message through telepathy, to deserving aspirants in the different corners of the world. Means of communication that are supernormal to us are quite normal to a Yogi.

Influence Others by Thought

❖ You can influence another man without any audible language. What is needed is concentration of thought that is directed by the will. This is telepathy.

❖ Try this. Think of your friend or cousin who is living in a distant land. Bring a clear-cut image of his face to your mind. If you have his photo, look at it and speak to it audibly. When you retire to bed think of the picture with intense concentration.

Your friend will write to you the desired letter the following day or so. Try this.

❖ Thought-vibrations travel faster than light or electricity. In such instances, the subconscious mind receives the messages or impressions and transmits the same to the conscious mind.

Varied Utility of Thought-Power

❖ The power of thought is very great. Every thought of yours has a literal value to you in every possible way. The strength of your body, the strength of your mind, your success in life, and the pleasures you give to others by your company — all depend on the nature and quality of your thoughts. You must know thought-culture, and develop thought-power.

The Value of Thought-Power

❖ Unfold the occult powers hidden within you by understanding and realising the powers of the mind. Close your eyes and concentrate. You can see distant objects, hear distant sounds, send messages to any part of the world, and heal persons thousands of miles away from you.

Thoughts Accomplish Many a Mission

❖ If you send out a loving, helpful thought to another man, it leaves your brain, goes directly to that person, raises a similar thought of love in his/her mind and returns to you with redoubled force.

❖ If you send out a thought of hatred to another person, it hurts that person and hurts you also by turning back to you with redoubled force.

❖ Therefore, understand the laws of thought; raise only thoughts of mercy, love and kindness from your mind, and be happy always.

Parapsychology and Subconscious Thoughts

- Practice of telepathy, thought-reading, hypnotism, mesmerism and psychic-healing clearly proves that the mind exists and that a higher mind can influence and subjugate the lower mind. From the automatic writing and the experiences of a hypnotised person, we can clearly infer the existence of the subconscious mind which operates throughout the twenty-four hours of the day.

Power of Vigorous, Divine Thoughts

❖ Thought is life. What you think, that you are. Your thought creates your environment. Your thoughts constitute your world.

❖ If you entertain healthy thoughts, you can keep good health. If you hold on to sickly thoughts in the mind, thoughts of diseased tissues, thoughts of weak nerves, thoughts of improper functioning of organs, you can never expect good health, beauty and harmony.

- ❖ Remember that the body is a product of the mind and is under the control of the mind.
- ❖ If you hold on to vigorous thoughts, your body, too, will be vigorous. Thoughts of love, peace, contentment purity, perfection and divinity makes you, and also others around you, perfect and Divine. Cultivate divine thoughts.

Every good thought sent out rebounds a hundred times with its force, on the sender himself; so too do bad thoughts.

The only private treasure we can really possess in this world is our own thoughts within. It is a sacred sanctum and none can invade it.

The source of all evil,
like a tree from a seed,
starts from our own wrong thinking
or false imagination.
Thought is creative.
It can make or unmake us.

– Swami Chinmayananda

Thoughts Promote Radiant Health

❖ The body is internally associated with the mind, rather the body is a counterpart of the mind. It is a gross visible form of the subtle, invisible mind. If there is pain in the tooth or in the stomach or in the ear, the mind is at once affected. It ceases to think properly; it is agitated, disturbed and perturbed.

❖ If there is depression in the mind, the body also cannot function properly.

Pains which afflict the body are called the secondary diseases (*Vyadhi*) while the desires (*Vasanas*) that afflict the mind are termed mental or primary diseases (*Adhi*).

❖ If the mind is healthy, the body will necessarily be healthy. If the mind is pure, if your thoughts are pure, you will be free from all diseases.

Thoughts Develop Personality

❖ Those who have a little control over their thoughts and speech will have a calm, serene, beautiful, charming face and a sweet voice, and their eyes will turn brilliant and lustrous.

Thoughts Cause Physiological Disorders

❖ Every change in thought makes a vibration in your mental body and this, when transmitted to the physical body, causes activity in the nervous matter of your brain. This activity in the nervous cells causes many electrical and chemical changes in them. It is thought-activity which causes these changes.

❖ Passion, hatred, longstanding bitterness jealousy, corroding anxiety, and fits of hot temper actually destroy the cells of the body.

More gold has been mined from the thoughts of men than has ever been taken from the earth.
– Anonymous

Acquisition of Thought-Power by Moral Purity

- A man who speaks the truth and has moral purity has powerful thoughts always.
- Virtues like truthfulness, earnestness and industry are the best sources of mental power.

Thought-power by Concentration

- There is no limit to the power of human thought. The more concentrated the human mind is, the more power is brought to bear on one point.

- ❖ The rays of the mind are scattered in the case of the worldly-minded person. There is dissipation of mental energy in various directions. For the purpose of concentration, these scattered rays have to be gathered by the practice of concentration.

Thought-Power by Organised Thinking

❖ Destroy random thinking. Take a subject and think of its different aspects and bearing. Never allow any other thought to enter the conscious mind.

Thought-power by Will-power

❖ Every sensual thought rejected, every temptation resisted, every harsh word withheld, every noble aspiration encouraged, helps you to develop will-power or soul-force.

❖ The will is the dynamic soul-force. When it operates, all mental powers, such as the power of judgement, the power of memory, the power of grasping, the power of reasoning, the power of reflection and inference, all come into instant play.

Simple Prescriptions for Clear Thinking

❖ Think clearly. Clarify your ideas again and again. Introspect in solitude. Purify your thoughts to a considerable degree.

❖ Do not allow the mind to bubble. Let one thought-wave rise and settle down calmly. Then allow another thought to enter. Drive off all extraneous thoughts that have no connection with the subject-matter you are handling at a given moment.

Develop Individuality: Resist Suggestions

❖ Do not be easily influenced by the suggestions of others. Have your own sense of individuality.

Creative Imagination

❖ It is the faculty of mind through which 'hunches' and 'inspirations' are received. It is through this faculty that one individual may 'tune in' or communicate with the sub-conscious minds of other men.

❖ Even the 'genius' draws upon this ability when he is unable to solve a problem through his normal potentialities.

— *Napolean Hill*

Gems of Wisdom from Sri Sathya Sai Baba

❖ Do not give all your thoughts immediate expression; select, ponder and then speak out.

❖ Every thought, scene and occasion leaves an impression on the mind; be ever on the alert that contact with evil thought is avoided.

❖ As one feels, so he becomes. As are the thoughts, so are the results. As is the seed, so is the plant. As is the flour, so is the bread.

❖ The mind is the breeding ground of all thoughts. It collects and treasures every impression created by the senses and it very easily is enslaved by glitter and glamour. It seldom weighs the pros and cons.

❖ Detach yourselves from the senses; only then can the soul *(atma)* shine. I do not mean that you should destroy the senses. The mind must be withdrawn from its present comrades, the senses. It must be loyal to its real master, the intellect *(buddhi)*.

❖ When the mind is controlling the senses, you experience lasting joy; when the senses become the masters, you are dragged into the dust.

❖ The senses must be kept under strict control by rigorous training; otherwise they will drag man away from his higher purpose.

❖ Perhaps you think it is not easy to control the senses. Even if it is not easy to control them, it is quite easy to divert all of them in the direction of God, and give them a new orientation.

Control of the Senses

Senses controlled can guard you against a host of evil. Man should avoid errors and evil that the ear, the tongue, the eye, the mind and the hand are liable to commit. The eye has a tendency to seek the vile and vulgar. It must be held in check so that it may not ruin the body as well as the mind. The ear is ever eager for scandals and gossip. It does not encourage you to hear spiritual discourses, but if someone is slandering another person, the two ears attain the maximum concentration. The tongue is extremely dangerous, and if not held in check it will continuously pour out scandals. When you can keep in check the eye, ear and tongue, then the mind and the hand can also be used for self-improvement.

Controlling One's Thoughts

Bad Thoughts

Sri Aurobindo says that all that one thinks one is, one can, by the very fact of that thinking, become. This knowledge of the fact that *all* that one thinks one can be, is an important key to the development of the being.

This makes us understand the necessity of not admitting into ourselves any thought which destroys aspiration or the creation of the truth of our being. It reveals the considerable importance of not allowing what one does not want to be or does not want to do, to formulate itself into thought within the being. Because to think these things is already a beginning of their realisation.

Sri Aurobindo says that thought is not the cause of existence but an intermediary, the instrument which gives form to life, to creation, and the control of this instrument is of foremost importance if one wants disorder and all that is anti-divine to disappear from creation.

One must not admit bad thoughts into oneself under the pretext that they are merely thoughts. They are tools of execution. And one should not allow them to exist in oneself if one does not want them to do their work of destruction.

On How to Get Rid of Unpleasant Thoughts

Generally, the easiest way to get rid of unpleasant thoughts is to think of something else. That is, to concentrate one's attention upon something that has nothing to do with that thought, has no connection with that thought, like reading or some work — generally, some creative work. Take the example of a writer. While he is writing, all other thoughts are gone, for he is concentrated on what he is doing. When he finishes writing, if he has no control, the other thoughts will return. So, precisely when one is attacked by a thought, one can try to do some creative work. Those who have begun to control their thoughts can make a movement of rejection, push aside the thought as one would a physical object. But that is more difficult and asks for a much greater mastery. Yet if you chase it off effectively and constantly or almost repeatedly, finally it does not come any more.

The third means is to be able to bring down a sufficiently great light from above which will be the "denial" in the deeper sense; that is, if the thought which comes is something dark, if one can bring down from above the light of true knowledge, a higher power, and put that light upon the thought, one can manage to dissolve it or enlighten or transform it – this is the supreme method. This is still a little more difficult. But it can be done, and if one does it, one is cured — not only does the thought not come back but the very cause is removed.

— *The Mother*

The Power of Positive Thinking

❖ Norman Vincent Peal has spent his lifetime emphasising the value of positive thinking through his numerous books. Dr Robert Schuller uses the term 'Possibility Thinking' to convey the same message.

❖ Positive thoughts provide the key to successful living as it is the positive attitude in life which makes our actions positive, a prerequisite for result-oriented performance.

- ❖ "When the going gets tough, the tough gets going", is a well known saying. All that is required to achieve your goal is to have faith in yourself. **Positive Mental Attitude** (PMA) has a lot to contribute not only towards goal achievement but also to generate a happy and enthusiastic atmosphere around you.

- ❖ The man who wins is the one who thinks he can. PMA can be achieved by the intricate and intimate interaction between the stimuli, emotions and motivation which can be controlled through your thought process. What is to be remembered is that positive emotions and positive actions can only result from positive thoughts. Suppression of negative thoughts, arousal of positive emotions and spreading enthusiasm all around, is what PMA is all about.

Advantages of PMA

- Organisational and individual goals are achieved.
- The right motivation generates enthusiasm to produce quality output.
- Maximum utilisation of mind power is achieved, which otherwise remains untapped.
- Positive emotions keep body's chemical exchanges in perfect balance and provide good health.
- The mind is trained to overcome difficult hurdles, in a positive fashion.

Practice of Positive Thinking

❖ In order to practise PMA, it is important to know the human mind mechanism. In outline, the process is :

- Stimuli are received from the environment or internally.

- These are perceived by our five senses. Impulses are then sent to the brain.

- Human thoughts appraise the impulses as good, bad or neutral.

- The thoughts in turn cause physiological and chemical reactions in the body to generate action.

❖ During the process of PMA, it is necessary to ensure that the right actions result. The thought appraisal needs to be toned up to accept good impulses, reject bad ones and ignore ones of neutral category. A three step simple formula is:
- ◆ Strive to achieve success because you feel a driving need to excel.
- ◆ Focus on a particular task which you feel is likely to bring success.

- Believe in yourself and in a singular thought that success will be yours.
- Some of the simple techniques which can generate positive emotions and positive thoughts are:

Choose Positive Stimuli

Remember, you feel and act as you Think. So, be selective in what you read or listen. If inputs to the mind are positive, so will be the output. Associate yourself with positive, cheerful and optimistic people.

Select Positive Words

❖ Avoid "I", and talk of "You" and "We".

❖ Do not use the word "No" at the beginning of a sentence during a conversation. Try and convey the same thing positively.

❖ The use of "If" creates doubts and conveys negative feelings. Say "when"...

❖ Do not start your conversation by saying..., "I do not agree with you." Just express your opinion on the subject.

- ❖ Never use the word "Impossible"; it only paralyses your creative power.

Prefer Positive Talk

Make an effort to arouse positive feelings of love, friendliness and enthusiasm. Some useful tips are :

- ❖ Greet everyone warmly. Do not consider relative rank or status when you meet some one.
- ❖ Talk good of everybody. Follow the dictum :

  See no evil; Hear no evil; speak no evil.

❖ Positive affirmation boosts positive emotions. When you wake up in the morning, and also several times during the day, say enthusiastically to yourself, "This is a new day for new health and new success. I feel dynamic."

❖ Use the present tense and not the future tense. Suppose you have a headache. Do not say, "My headache will go." It only reinforces your headache. Say something like, "My head is clear, perfectly clear."

Enjoy Inspiring Songs

Start the day on a positive note. It should be refreshing and inspiring. The song could be a simple one like - "Pack up your troubles in your old kit bag and smile, smile, smile...."

Smile and Laugh More

- ❖ Laughter is really the best medicine. It not only cures you but also all around you.
- ❖ A hearty laugh does wonders to your mind and body and surprisingly takes only one fifth of muscle power than that of a good frown.

- ❖ Develop a sense of humour and learn to laugh at your imperfections.
- ❖ Smile more and more. Remember, man is the only animal capable of doing it.

Look for Positivity in Everything

- ❖ Perceive a half glass, as half filled and not half empty.
- ❖ Look for an opportunity in every adversity. There is always something to learn.
- ❖ Act like a sun dial — count only your sunny hours.

Do Not Stay Depressed

Even if you are down in the dumps — do not remain there. Try some of these simple steps:

❖ Use the stop/cancel technique. You may wonder how you can stop thinking of something that is bothering you. With practice, it is possible. With practice it is possible to switch your thoughts to a pleasant memory of an outstanding achievement of yours. In a fraction of a second you feel the depressing thoughts melting away.

- ❖ Get busy in some absorbing activity.
- ❖ Practise relaxation.

Let Go Your Gloomy Thoughts

❖ Carefully watch all your thoughts. Suppose you are assailed by gloomy thoughts, find out the cause for the depression and try to remove the cause.

❖ The best method to overcome gloomy thoughts and consequent depression, is to think of inspiring thoughts and inspiring things.

❖ Singing is very beneficial to drive off gloom. Chant God's name loudly several times. Run in the open air. The depression will vanish soon. This is the easiest method.

- If there is a feeling of anger, think of love. If there are thoughts of jealousy, think of the advantages of charitableness and magnanimity.
- If there is harshness of heart, think of mercy. If there is lust, think of the advantage of celibacy. If there is dishonesty think of honesty, integrity. If there is miserliness, think of generosity and generous people.

❖ If there is infatuation, think of discrimination; if there is pride, think of humility, if there is hypocrisy, think of frankness and its invaluable advantages, and if there is timidity, think of courage.

The Power of Thought

- There is nothing either good or bad, but thinking makes it so.

  – Shakespeare

- Great thoughts reduced to practice become great acts.

  – Hazlitt

- Imagination is more important than knowledge.

  – Einstein

- Be careful of what you think you want in life, because you'll get it.

  – Anon

Positive Methods for Thought-Control

Thought-Control through Concentration

❖ When irrelevant thoughts enter the mind, be indifferent. They will pass away. Do not drive them out forcibly. They will persist and resist. But substitute it with divine thoughts. Irrelevant thoughts will gradually fade out. Be slow and steady in the practice of concentration.

❖ It is easy to concentrate the mind on external objects. The mind has a natural tendency to go outwards. Keep the picture of your God in front of you. Look at it steadily without blinking. When your mind calms down, close your eyes and mentally visualise the picture.

❖ You should be able to visualise the picture very clearly even in its absence. You will have to call up the mental picture at a moment's notice. Keep it there steadily for sometime. This is concentration. You will have to practise this daily.

- ❖ If you want to increase your powers of concentration, you will have to reduce your worldly desires and activities. You will have to observe silence every day for some hours. Then only can the mind concentrate easily and without difficulty.

- ❖ In concentration you will have only one thought. The mind assumes the form of only one object. All other operations of the mind are suspended.

Thought-Control by Non-Cooperation

❖ Do not cooperate with the mind in its evil wanderings. Gradually the mind will come under your control. Here is the practical method towards non-cooperation with the mind. If the mind says : "I must eat sweetmeats today", say to the mind: "I will not cooperate with you today, I will not eat sweetmeats. I will eat only bread and pulses." Non-cooperation with the mind is swimming against the sensual currents. Gradually you will gain mastery over the mind.

Art of Thinning out Thoughts

❖ Passion, egoism, jealousy, pride and hatred are very deep-rooted. If you cut the branches of a tree, they grow again after sometime. Even so, these thoughts that are suppressed manifest themselves again after sometime. They should be completely rooted out by strenuous efforts, meditation, etc.

❖ Napoleon controlled his thoughts in this manner : "When I want to think of things more pleasant, I close the cupboards of my mind revealing the more unpleasant things of life, and open up the cupboards containing the more pleasant thoughts. If I want to sleep, I close up all the cupboards of my mind!"

Give Wrong Thoughts No Concession

- ❖ At first a wrong thought enters the mind. Then the imagination begins to take control. You take delight in dwelling on the wrong thoughts.
- ❖ You give consent to its stay in the mind, and gradually the wrong thought, when it is not resisted, takes a strong hold of your mind.
- ❖ Then it becomes very difficult to drive it off. The proverb goes : "Give a rogue an inch, and he will take a yard." This is true of wrong thoughts also.

Nip Bad Thoughts in the Bud

❖ Just as you close your door or gate when a dog or an ass tries to come in, similarly close your mind before any evil thought can enter and leave an impression on your physical brain. You will become wise soon and attain eternal, infinite peace and bliss.

❖ Wipe out lust, greed and egoism. Entertain only pure holy thoughts. This is an uphill task. You will have to practise it. You will succeed in your attempt after sometime.

- ❖ Destruction of one bad thought will give you strength to annihilate other thoughts and will develop your soul-force or will-power.

- ❖ Never despair though you may fail in crushing a bad thought. No pains, no gains. Inner spiritual strength will gradually manifest itself in you. You can feel this.

Best Remedies for Evil Thoughts

❖ Keep the mind fully occupied. Then evil thoughts will not enter. An idle mind is the devil's workshop. Watch the mind every minute.

Avoid Thoughts of Another Man's Defects

❖ The nature of the mind is such that it becomes that which it intensely thinks of. Thus if you think of the vices and defects of other people, your mind will be charged with these vices and defects at least for the time being.

- ❖ He who knows this psychological law will never indulge in censuring others or in finding fault with the conduct of others, but will see only the good in others, and will always praise others.

Thought, Energy and Sacred Thoughts

- ❖ Sacred thoughts generate and sustain divine thoughts. Thought moves. Thought decides the future. Thought makes a man a saint or a sinner. Thoughts can shape a man.

❖ Negative, evil thoughts cannot overcome fear. Patience overcomes anger and irritability. Love overcomes hatred. Purity overcomes lust.

From Pure Thoughts to Transcendental Experience

❖ Thoughts are of two kinds: pure thoughts and impure thoughts. Desire to do virtuous actions, *Japa*, meditation, study of religious books, etc., is pure thought. The desire to go to see a vulgar movie, to hurt others and to seek extramarital sex-relations, are impure thoughts.

Thought-Power and Practical Idealism

❖ Your thought is endowed with creative power. It can evolve objects from within itself. It is the only creator. Nothing ever will be created or recreated except through the mind. Thought is the material out of which things are made. All matter is but materialisation of the consciousness.

❖ The world around you is only what you believe it to be. Your perceptions are coloured by your thoughts. Your mind perceives and continues to perceive the things in that very form in which it imagines it to be with full faith. Pierce through the steel-armour of biased thoughts, and try to see the divinity in every object.

❖ Develop a pure mind and whatever objects and worlds you wish to get, you will gain those objects and worlds.

❖ Develop strong determination. It is an important factor which will contribute to the realisation of your thoughts. There is nobody who will be able to withstand the power of your determined mind.

- Every depressing and disturbing thought that enters your brain, has a depressing effect on every cell of your body, and tends to produce disease. All negative thoughts are forerunners of disease, and they are messengers of death.

- If you want to live long and lead a sensible and healthy life, cherish good thoughts. Subtle and powerful are the influences of thoughts in the building and rebuilding of your body. Be vigilant.

- Every good thought stimulates the heart, improves the digestive system and promotes the normal action of every gland.

❖ Contentment is another name for the harmony of the mind. When your thoughts do not wander to this or that object, and when you feel self-satisfied, you are in a state of joy which is unique. If you are happy within, everything appears good and pleasing to you.

❖ Let the mind turn towards the spiritual. Your mind will be at peace. You will enjoy excellent mental and physical well-being.

— Swami Sivananda